Early
Domestic
Architecture
of
Pennsylvania

Outbuilding with Red Tile Roof, Berks County

Early Domestic Architecture of Pennsylvania

Photographs and Measured Drawings

by

Eleanor Raymond A.I.A.

with an Introduction by
R. Brognard Okie

4880 Lower Valley Road, Atglen, PA 19310 USA

Published by Schiffer Publishing Ltd.
4880 Lower Valley Road
Atglen, PA 19310
Phone: (610) 593-1777; Fax: (610) 593-2002
E-mail: Info@schifferbooks.com

For the largest selection of fine reference books on this and related subjects, please visit our web
site at **www.schifferbooks.com**
We are always looking for people to write books on new and related subjects. If you have an idea
for a book please contact us at the above address.

This book may be purchased from the publisher.
Include $3.95 for shipping.
Please try your bookstore first.
You may write for a free catalog.

In Europe, Schiffer books are distributed by
Bushwood Books
6 Marksbury Ave.
Kew Gardens
Surrey TW9 4JF England
Phone: 44 (0) 20 8392-8585; Fax: 44 (0) 20 8392-9876
E-mail: info@bushwoodbooks.co.uk
Website: www.bushwoodbooks.co.uk
Free postage in the U.K., Europe; air mail at cost.

FOREWORD

SO much attention is being directed to-day toward the so-called 'modern' movement in the arts, that the publication of a book on the early architecture of Pennsylvania may seem on first thought a superfluous and untimely gesture of appreciation of our architectural traditions with no constructive application to the present or the future. However, observation of the modern movement, both abroad and at home, and a close study of these old Pennsylvania buildings will clearly show that the motives and ideals of both are the same. To perceive how sincerely these houses and farm buildings manifest their function, how perfectly they are adapted to site and how simply they are expressed in the best materials at hand is only to recall that these qualities are the identical ones exemplified by all the great architectural movements of the past.

An unstudied directness in fitting form to function, which seems to have been guided by an instinctive appreciation of proportion, and by skill in the use of materials have then resulted in the excellent design shown in these buildings. Such simple expedients as the shade value of a tree over the spring house; the desirability of a separate summer kitchen and bake oven exacted by the warm summer climate; the need of the individual smoke house and slaughter house indispensable to a self-supporting farm; the necessity for a barn extensive enough to hold the crops and live stock of a large, fertile, expertly cultivated farm and to provide a threshing floor for the grain; the demand for a place to mend the harness and perform other sitting chores in the open air while protected from the hot sun and rain—these and other practical considerations have been determining factors in the development of the characteristics peculiar to these buildings. The abundance of unusually beautiful and structurally valuable stone found on every hand is responsible for the frequency with which we find this material used in the early buildings. And this stonework so beautifully laid on its natural horizontal bed that it has ignored the ravages of almost three hundred years and will endure for many generations to come, is of unrivalled excellence.

In choosing the buildings for this book I have been guided solely by the architectural value of the subject, and have attempted to indicate the great variety of treatment found in the same type of building as well as the full range of minor buildings. I have not been actuated by historical or archaeological interests. In most cases the buildings chosen have not been published before. The period covered is from the settlement of Pennsylvania through the early Georgian, a period more extensive in some localities than others and hence not definable by dates since many characteristics of an earlier period will be found carried along for generations in remote districts or for special uses. In the main I have included only such buildings as show traces of the mediaeval spirit or early Georgian character such as the cove cornice or pent eave so characteristic of the locality. The fully developed Georgian building has been excluded as being worth of a book in itself.

I wish to acknowledge with sincerest appreciation my debt to Miss Ruth Crook, my field scout, for her devotion and skill in performing the arduous task of hunting down most of the material I have used, and of photographing and measuring much of it. It has taken over five months of constant searching to find these buildings, which lie scattered over the eastern part of Pennsylvania from Harrisburg to Philadelphia. While the material is prolific, much of it is hidden away where a less zealous hunter than Miss Crook would have failed to find it and much more of it has been ruined by later alterations or additions and so rendered useless for our purpose. The illustrations selected for the book were culled from over a thousand photographs which were taken during the course of an eight thousand mile tour in a trusty Ford.

In acknowledging other sources of help in the preparation of this book I mention first that of Mr. R. Brognard Okie, Architect, whose invaluable suggestions and enthusiastic endorsement of what we were doing furnished the motive power sometimes needed. In the same category I place Mr. Charles B. Montgomery, curator of the Historical Society of Berks County, who gave unstintingly of his time and knowledge in helping us find some of the best of our material. For the encouragement of Mr. Fiske Kimball, Director of the Philadelphia Museum of Fine Arts, for the patient cooperation of Mr. P. B. Wallace of Philadelphia, who took many of the photographs for the book, and for the generosity of the Harrisburg State Library in giving permission to use their photographs of the Ephrata Cloister, I also am very grateful.

ELEANOR RAYMOND

INTRODUCTION

THERE have been a number of books published illustrating the early buildings in Pennsylvania. The authors of these books have not thought it worth while to show the smaller or more primitive houses or the barns and out-buildings that are so typical of Eastern Pennsylvania in particular, and that add so much to the attractiveness of the countryside.

It should be rather humiliating to some of us who are so fond of the simple type of buildings but have done nothing to make a lasting record of them, that Miss Raymond (a Boston Architect) has stolen a march on us by putting in book form a record of interior and exterior views, not only of the smaller houses but of barns, mills, spring houses and other out-buildings which are fast disappearing from our countryside.

As we travel through the country we are impressed with the good judgment and the artistic sense which those who first located the houses and the various out-buildings used in selecting sites for them.

It is remarkable how cleverly they located the house itself and each of the buildings around the house, and the relation of one to the other. We should have in mind also the fact that at that time there was not anything like so much cleared land as at present; the original sites being many of them forested, making the selection of a site much more difficult.

To illustrate conditions when some of the earlier houses were built, the photographs of Fort Zeller near Womelsdorf show a house used as a fort in the event of an Indian attack and the story is that the farmer's wife killed three Indians, one after the other, dragging them inside the door.

In a number of the illustrations, the original house has been enlarged by an extension either at one side, at the back, or at the front. In some cases the spring house, shop or wagon house was the original dwelling, the present house being put up by a later generation.

One of the chief charms of these old buildings is the natural way in which they fit the ground. Whether on the side of a hill with entrance doors at both upper and lower levels, or with practically flat ground around the house the effect is invariably restful and inviting.

EARLY DOMESTIC ARCHITECTURE OF PENNSYLVANIA

Those who built these old buildings, whether of stone, brick, logs or frame, had certainly a keen sense of proportion. They knew exactly where to place their doors and windows, and how to design their cornices; and whether the roof pitches were steep as in the earlier houses or flatter as in the later ones they look just right and could to good advantage be more often heeded today. It is a fact that the old buildings existing today are beautifully proportioned, even the simplest woodshed or spring house or bake oven having a charm of its own. Often the simpler the house the more interesting the arrangement of small wall cupboards, boxed-in stairs, and so forth, and the ingenious use made of space that in the larger houses would be wasted.

The interiors are, if anything, more fascinating than the exteriors and not only show what a thorough knowledge of native timber these men had and how to frame it, but are a testimony of the skill and accuracy with which the carpenters and other mechanics did their work. Their work shows that they enjoyed doing it.

We are apt to hear it remarked that you cannot get material today such as these old time mechanics used. Perhaps this is true but today's woodwork would last much longer if put together as it was done one hundred and fifty to two hundred years ago.

When we examine the interior of these old houses carefully, we find that not only is each house different, but no two rooms in any house are exactly alike, each having individual details of door or window trim, mantels, stairways, and so forth, that give a charm and interest to the interiors entirely lacking in so much of the modern work.

There are also characteristic details and methods typical of certain localities that it is most interesting to note, showing the influence of a master builder or mechanic in that locality. This is true not only as regards carpenter work but also with the hand-wrought hardware that is in many instances still in position and perfect working order. It is also apparent but to a lesser degree in stone work and in painting.

The combination of wood and plaster is also typical of the period and shows that these men well understood how to get a more pleasing relation of wood and plaster surfaces. The wood finish was put in place before plastering was done and served as a ground or surface to which the plaster was made flush or about flush at completion. Just the right amount of plaster was used to enhance the value and beauty of the wood surfaces of either painted or moulded or plain beaded boards. The stone walls or split oak lath to which the plaster was applied provided a backing which assured a finished surface neither harsh nor too mechanical.

It would be a pity not to particularly mention the grist mills, a few examples of which Miss Raymond has fortunately been able to illustrate, and none too soon, as the few that remain of these fine old buildings are fast disappearing.

The mills combine the nice fitting to the ground and feeling for proportion of the houses with the desire for durability and sturdiness of the farm barns. The timber framing of the mills and the use made in their construction of white oak, yellow poplar and white pine is a study in itself. No mill was complete without its miller's office with wide board floors, fireplace, and a combination of wood and plastered walls, all as simple as possible and the more pleasing for being so.

Miss Raymond has done a real service in making a permanent record of these fine old buildings in such an instructive and interesting way. It is to be hoped that she has derived a proportion at least of the pleasure in her work the illustrations will give to others.

R. BROGNARD OKIE

August, 1930.
Philadelphia, Pennsylvania.

LIST OF PLATES

EARLY DOMESTIC ARCHITECTURE OF PENNSYLVANIA

LIST OF PLATES

LIST OF PLATES

LIST OF PLATES

LIST OF PLATES

FARM OUTBUILDINGS—SPRING HOUSES, SMOKE HOUSES AND BAKE HOUSES

LIST OF PLATES

LIST OF PLATES

LIST OF PLATES

LIST OF PLATES

PLATE 1

THE CLOISTER, EPHRATA, LANCASTER COUNTY

PLATE 2

Photographs, Courtesy of the State Library, Harrisburg

THE CLOISTER, EPHRATA, LANCASTER COUNTY

PLATE 3

Photographs, Courtesy of the State Library, Harrisburg

THE CLOISTER, EPHRATA, LANCASTER COUNTY

PLATE 4

THE KITCHEN

MAIN DOORWAY, SISTER HOUSE

INTERIOR DOOR

THE CLOISTER, EPHRATA, LANCASTER COUNTY

PLATE 5

INTERIOR OF THE SAAL, EPHRATA, LANCASTER COUNTY

PLATE 6

STAIR LANDING

FIREPLACE

MAIN STAIRWAY

FIREPLACE—DATE 1728

SISTER HOUSE, THE CLOISTER, EPHRATA, LANCASTER COUNTY

PLATE 7

THE CLOISTER, EPHRATA, LANCASTER COUNTY

PLATE 8

See Measured Drawing, Plate 148

THIRD FLOOR FIREPLACE—DATE 1728

See Measured Drawing, Plate 149

SECOND FLOOR FIREPLACE—DATE 1728

SISTER HOUSE, THE CLOISTER, EPHRATA, LANCASTER COUNTY

PLATE 9

WALL CONSTRUCTION

ROOF CONSTRUCTION. NOTE AIR SPACE
BETWEEN PLASTER AND SHINGLE
STRIPS

Photographs, Courtesy of the State Library, Harrisburg

CHIMNEY IN ATTIC

THE CLOISTER, EPHRATA, LANCASTER COUNTY

PLATE 10

MUHLENBERG CHURCH, TRAPPE, MONTGOMERY COUNTY

PLATE 11

Date 1743

Augustus Lutheran Church, Trappe, Montgomery County

PLATE 12

Date 1743

AUGUSTUS LUTHERAN CHURCH, TRAPPE, MONTGOMERY COUNTY

PLATE 13

AUGUSTUS LUTHERAN CHURCH, TRAPPE, MONTGOMERY COUNTY

PLATE 14

MENNONITE MEETING HOUSE, LANDISVILLE, LANCASTER COUNTY

OLD MEETING HOUSE ON PAXTANG ROAD, LANCASTER COUNTY

PLATE 15

EXETER FRIENDS MEETING HOUSE, OLEY VALLEY, BERKS COUNTY

OCTAGONAL BUILDING FORMERLY A SCHOOL HOUSE, NEWTOWN, CHESTER COUNTY

PLATE 16

EARLY DOMESTIC ARCHITECTURE OF PENNSYLVANIA

BRIDGE AT MARTINDALE, LANCASTER COUNTY

COVERED BRIDGE AND CATTLE RUN NEAR HINKLETOWN,
LANCASTER COUNTY

PLATE 17

BRIDGE ACROSS THE PERKIOMEN AT COLLEGEVILLE, MONTGOMERY COUNTY

BRIDGE ACROSS THE BRANDYWINE AT MARSHALLTON, CHESTER COUNTY

Plate 18

The Flume at Green Bank Mill, Lancaster County

PLATE 19

GRIST MILL AT MORTONVILLE, CHESTER COUNTY

OLD FOREBAY AND MODERN WATER
WHEEL ON THE OLD CONESTOGA ROAD,
CHESTER COUNTY

DETAIL OF OLD WOODEN WATER WHEEL,
LEHIGH COUNTY

PLATE 20

GENERAL VIEW

DOORWAY

MILL NEAR PEACH BOTTOM, LANCASTER COUNTY

PLATE 21

INTERIOR OF STONE ROADS MILL ON THE LITTLE CONESTOGA CREEK,
LANCASTER COUNTY

PLATE 22

FORT ZELLER NEAR WERNERSVILLE, LEBANON COUNTY

PLATE 23

EARLY DOMESTIC ARCHITECTURE OF PENNSYLVANIA

ENTRANCE DOOR

DOOR TO SPRING ROOM

FORT ZELLER NEAR WERNERSVILLE, LEBANON COUNTY

PLATE 24

EARLY DOMESTIC ARCHITECTURE OF PENNSYLVANIA

STAIRS

See Measured Drawing, Plate 149 KITCHEN FIREPLACE

FORT ZELLER NEAR WERNERSVILLE, LEBANON COUNTY

PLATE 25

WINDOW IN SPRING ROOM—EXTERIOR VIEW

WINDOW IN SPRING ROOM—INTERIOR VIEW

FRAMING IN SPRING ROOM

INTERIOR DOOR

FORT ZELLER NEAR WERNERSVILLE, LEBANON COUNTY

PLATE 26

VALENDINE VIHMANN HOUSE NEAR MILLBACH, LEBANON COUNTY

PETER BRICKNER HOUSE, COCALICO MILLS,
LANCASTER COUNTY

VALENDINE VIHMANN HOUSE NEAR
MILLBACH, LEBANON COUNTY

PLATE 27

INTERIOR DOOR

SOLID RAILING OF STAIR WELL, SECOND FLOOR

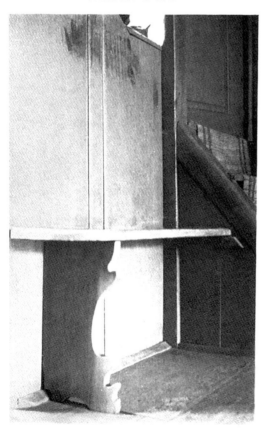

STAIR AND SEAT

ENTRANCE AND ENCLOSED STAIR

VALENDINE VIHMANN HOUSE NEAR MILLBACH, LEBANON COUNTY

Plate 28

Date 1776

House on the Estate of Percy Chandler, Esq., at Chadds Ford,
Chester County

PLATE 29

See Measured Drawing, Plate 138   PARLOR

See Measured Drawing, Plate 139

WEST BED ROOM

HOUSE ON THE ESTATE OF PERCY CHANDLER, ESQ., AT CHADDS FORD,
CHESTER COUNTY

PLATE 30

See Measured Drawing, Plate 138

HOUSE ON THE ESTATE OF PERCY CHANDLER, ESQ., AT CHADDS FORD,
CHESTER COUNTY

PLATE 31

EARLY DOMESTIC ARCHITECTURE OF PENNSYLVANIA

See Measured Drawing, Plate 141

REAR STAIR HALL

See Measured Drawing, Plate 141

HOUSE ON THE ESTATE OF PERCY CHANDLER, ESQ., AT CHADDS FORD, CHESTER COUNTY

PLATE 32

EXTERIOR VIEW

See Measured Drawing, Plate 145

KITCHEN FIREPLACE

GARRETT HOMESTEAD NEAR EDGEMONT, CHESTER COUNTY

PLATE 33

See Measured Drawing, Plate 14f   DETAILS OF FIREPLACE WALL

THE GRILL LIGHTS AN ENCLOSED STAIRWAY

GARRETT HOMESTEAD NEAR EDGEMONT, CHESTER COUNTY

PLATE 34

MAIN VIEW

STAIR LANDING   STAIRWAY TO THIRD FLOOR

PRIMITIVE HALL, CHATHAM, CHESTER COUNTY

PLATE 35

See Measured Drawing, Plate 144

STAIRWAY

PRIMITIVE HALL, CHATHAM, CHESTER COUNTY

PLATE 36

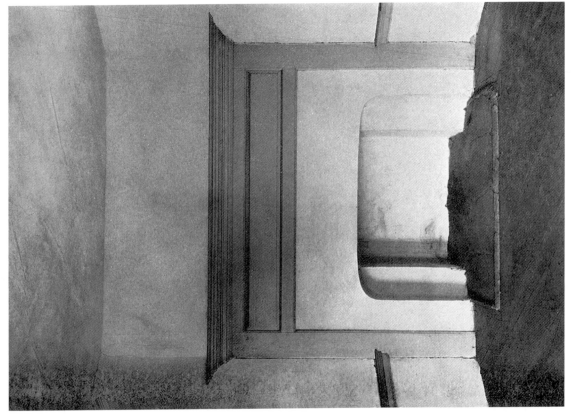

See Measured Drawing, Plate 142

See Measured Drawing, Plate 143

MANTELS

PRIMITIVE HALL, CHATHAM, CHESTER COUNTY

PLATE 37

EXTERIOR VIEW

INTERIOR VIEW

HOUSE AT CONCORDVILLE, DELAWARE COUNTY

PLATE 38

MANTELS

HOUSE AT CONCORDVILLE, DELAWARE COUNTY

PLATE 39

GENERAL VIEW

See Measured Drawing, Plate 136

THE KITCHEN

WARRENPOINT, CHESTER COUNTY

PLATE 40

FIRST FLOOR ROOM—DATE 1756

See Measured Drawing, Plate 135

PARLOR—DATE 1756

WARRENPOINT, CHESTER COUNTY

PLATE 41

See Measured Drawing, Plate 134

THE FRONT STAIRS—DATE 1756

WARRENPOINT, CHESTER COUNTY

PLATE 42

FIRST FLOOR ROOM

PARLOR

CUPBOARDS

WARRENPOINT, CHESTER COUNTY

PLATE 43

SOUTHEAST BEDROOM

NORTHWEST BEDROOM

WARRENPOINT, CHESTER COUNTY

PLATE 44

KITCHEN FIREPLACE, OLEY VALLEY, BERKS COUNTY

FIREPLACE, COLLINS HOUSE, CHESTER COUNTY

PLATE 45

KITCHEN FIREPLACE NEAR FRENCH CREEK, CHESTER COUNTY

Note Wooden Crane and Seat Built in at Right Hand End

KITCHEN FIREPLACE AT CONCORDVILLE, DELAWARE COUNTY

PLATE 46

See Measured Drawing, Plate 147   STAIRWAY

DOWNING HOUSE, DOWNINGTOWN, CHESTER COUNTY

See Measured Drawing, Plate 146   WINDOW

COVENTRY HOUSE, COVENTRYVILLE, CHESTER COUNTY

PLATE 47

COVENTRY HOUSE, COVENTRYVILLE, CHESTER COUNTY

MOUNT PLEASANT, THE BULL HOMESTEAD AT BULLTOWN, CHESTER COUNTY

PLATE 48

CUPBOARD

STAIRWAY

MOUNT PLEASANT, THE BULL HOMESTEAD AT BULLTOWN, CHESTER COUNTY

PLATE 49

HOUSE NEAR QUARRYVILLE,
LANCASTER COUNTY

CHRISTIAN HERR HOUSE,
LANCASTER COUNTY

HOUSE NEAR CHATHAM,
CHESTER COUNTY

FROM HOME OF AN EARLY WELSH
SETTLER IN CONESTOGA VALLEY

CORNER CUPBOARDS

PLATE 50

CORNER CUPBOARD IN FARMHOUSE
NEAR HAMMER CREEK, LANCASTER
COUNTY

CORNER CUPBOARD IN FARMHOUSE
NEAR READING, BERKS COUNTY

CORNER CUPBOARD IN PAXON HOUSE
SOLEBURY, BUCKS COUNTY

PLATE 51

See Measured Drawing, Plate 157

ROOF FRAMING IN FARMHOUSE IN THE TULPEHOCKEN, BERKS COUNTY

Plate 52

Date 1733

House of George Boone (Grandfather of Daniel Boone), in the Oley Valley,
Berks County

PLATE 53

BERTOLET HOUSE IN THE OLEY VALLEY, BERKS COUNTY

Note Trout Pool Between House and Spring House

OLD KAUFFMAN HOUSE IN THE OLEY VALLEY, BERKS COUNTY

PLATE 54

HOUSE ON THE ROAD BETWEEN STEVENS AND LINCOLN, LANCASTER COUNTY

HOUSE NEAR SCHAEFFERSTOWN, LEBANON COUNTY

PLATE 55

MAGEE HOUSE, FULTON TOWNSHIP, LANCASTER COUNTY

HOUSE ON THE VALLEY CREEK ROAD, CHESTER COUNTY

PLATE 56

REAR ELEVATION

See Measured Drawing, Plate 150

FRONT ELEVATION

BROWN HOUSE, PEACH BOTTOM, LANCASTER COUNTY

PLATE 57

SIDE ELEVATION

GENERAL VIEW

DOWNING HOUSE, DOWNINGTOWN, CHESTER COUNTY

PLATE 58

House at Brandywine Manor, Chester County

House near Chatham, Chester County

PLATE 59

REAR VIEW

GENERAL VIEW

HOUSE NEAR HAMMER CREEK IN ELIZABETH TOWNSHIP, LANCASTER COUNTY

PLATE 60

KNABB HOUSE IN THE OLEY VALLEY, BERKS COUNTY

HOUSE NORTH OF REFTON IN STRASBURG TOWNSHIP, LANCASTER COUNTY

PLATE 61

HOUSE AT DOUGLASSVILLE, BERKS COUNTY

MOUNT PLEASANT AT BULLTOWN, CHESTER COUNTY

PLATE 62

House at Compass, Chester County

West House at Whitemarsh, Montgomery County

Plate 63

General View

South Ell

Tenant House at Mount Pleasant, Bulltown, Chester County

PLATE 64

HOUSE NEAR BUCKINGHAM, BUCKS COUNTY

PLATE 65

Used as Lafayette's Headquarters During the Battle of the Brandywine

HOUSE ON THE BALTIMORE PIKE NEAR CHADDS FORD, CHESTER COUNTY

HOUSE ON THE BRANDYWINE NEAR
DOWNINGTOWN, CHESTER COUNTY

HOUSE NEAR DARLINGTON CORNERS
CHESTER COUNTY

PLATE 66

House Between Martindale and Hinkletown, Lancaster County

Old Bull House at Elverson, Chester County

PLATE 67

DARRAH HOUSE NEAR MANATAWNY CREEK, BERKS COUNTY

OLD TREXLER HOUSE, TREXLERTOWN, BERKS COUNTY

PLATE 68

TENANT HOUSE AT WARWICK FURNACE, CHESTER COUNTY

TWO VIEWS OF A HOUSE NEAR WEST CHESTER, CHESTER COUNTY

PLATE 69

Note Bake Oven at Left

REAR ELEVATION

See Measured Drawing, Plate 153

END ELEVATION

HOUSE AT SUGARTOWN, CHESTER COUNTY

PLATE 70

House on the Westover Road near Chadds Ford, Chester County

Two Views of a House near Cochranville, Chester County

PLATE 71

House on the Old York Road, York County

Outbuilding on Road from Carlisle to Shippensburg, Cumberland County

PLATE 72

Formerly a Toll-Gate House

HOUSE ON HORSESHOE PIKE NEAR DOWNINGTOWN,
CHESTER COUNTY

HOUSE AT MARTINDALE, LANCASTER COUNTY

PLATE 73

See Measured Drawing, Plate 154

HOUSE ON HORSESHOE PIKE NEAR DARLINGTOWN, CHESTER COUNTY

HOUSE NEAR MCCONNELLSBURG, FULTON COUNTY

PLATE 74

TENANT HOUSE NEAR OLEY, BERKS COUNTY

HOUSE NEAR PAOLI, CHESTER COUNTY

PLATE 75

House near Joanna Furnace, Berks County

House at Churchtown, Lancaster County

PLATE 76

HOUSE NEAR BUCKINGHAM, BUCKS COUNTY

HOUSE AT JOANNA FURNACE, BERKS COUNTY

PLATE 77

HOUSE IN JOANNA WOODLAND, BERKS COUNTY

HOUSE EAST OF BRANDYWINE MANOR,
CHESTER COUNTY

HOUSE NEAR BUCKTOWN ON THE
RIDGE ROAD, CHESTER COUNTY

PLATE 78

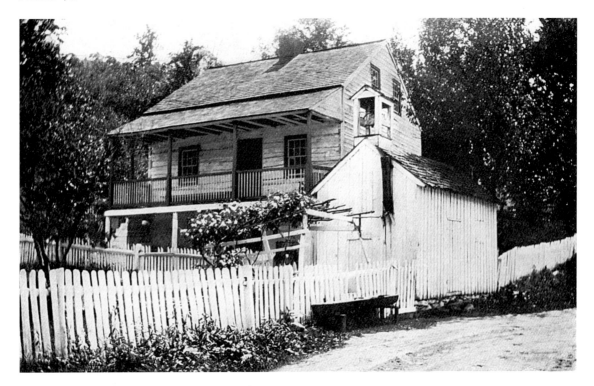

HOUSE NEAR MARTICVILLE, LANCASTER COUNTY

HOUSE IN THE FOREST, BERKS COUNTY

PLATE 79

HOUSE NEAR DOWNINGTOWN, CHESTER COUNTY

HOUSE AT CHURCHTOWN, LANCASTER COUNTY

PLATE 80

OUTBUILDING NEAR CHURCHTOWN, LANCASTER COUNTY

PLATE 81

UPPER LEVEL

LOWER LEVEL

SPRING AND TENANT HOUSE NEAR HINKLETOWN, LANCASTER COUNTY

PLATE 82

TOOL HOUSE, BERKS COUNTY

SPRING HOUSE, BERKS COUNTY

PLATE 83

Spring House near Downingtown, Chester County

Two Views of Spring House near Marshallton, Chester County

PLATE 84

OUTBUILDING ON FARM NEAR CHURCHTOWN,
LANCASTER COUNTY

SPRING HOUSE IN THE OLEY VALLEY, BERKS COUNTY

PLATE 85

GENERAL VIEW

ENTRANCE VIEW

OUTBUILDING AT PINE FORGE, BERKS COUNTY

PLATE 86

OUTBUILDING NEAR COLUMBIA, LANCASTER COUNTY

SPRING HOUSE NEAR MARSHALLTON, CHESTER COUNTY

Plate 87

Front Elevation

End Elevation

Spring House near White Horse, Chester County

PLATE 88

See Measured Drawing, Plate 155

SPRING HOUSE NEAR CHESTER SPRINGS, CHESTER COUNTY

SMOKE HOUSE AT SCHAEFFERSTOWN, LEBANON COUNTY

PLATE 89

See Measured Drawing, Plate 155

SPRING HOUSE NEAR CHESTER SPRINGS, CHESTER COUNTY

OUTBUILDING IN THE OLEY VALLEY, BERKS COUNTY

PLATE 90

SMOKE AND SPRING HOUSE AT BUCKTOWN,
CHESTER COUNTY

OUTBUILDING NEAR ST. DAVIDS, CHESTER COUNTY

PLATE 91

SPRING HOUSE, CHESTER COUNTY

PLATE 92

SPRING AND TENANT HOUSE, OLEY VALLEY, BERKS COUNTY

SMOKE HOUSE, LEBANON COUNTY

SMOKE HOUSE, OLEY VALLEY,
BERKS COUNTY

PLATE 93

SUMMER KITCHEN, BEARVILLE, LANCASTER COUNTY

BAKE OVEN IN THE OLEY VALLEY
BERKS COUNTY

BAKE OVEN AND ITS ROOF,
LANCASTER COUNTY

PLATE 94

SMALL BARN, BERKS COUNTY

CHICKEN HOUSE, BERKS COUNTY

SMALL BARN, BERKS COUNTY

WASH HOUSE, LANCASTER COUNTY

PLATE 95

MARTIC FORGE, LANCASTER COUNTY

BUCKS COUNTY

LANCASTER COUNTY

CHESTER COUNTY

SPRING HOUSES

PLATE 96

BARN NEAR MANATAWNY, BERKS COUNTY

SPANG'S BARN IN THE OLEY VALLEY, BERKS COUNTY

PLATE 97

FRONT ELEVATION

REAR ELEVATION

BARN ON THE KAUFFMAN FARM, OLEY VALLEY, BERKS COUNTY

PLATE 98

BARN AT FRIEDENSBURG, OLEY VALLEY, BERKS COUNTY

BARN NEAR READING, BERKS COUNTY

PLATE 99

FOREBAY OF BARN AT FRIEDENSBURG, OLEY VALLEY, BERKS COUNTY

BARN ON THE KAUFFMAN FARM, OLEY VALLEY, BERKS COUNTY

PLATE 100

BARN, COVENTRY HOUSE, COVENTRYVILLE,
BERKS COUNTY

BARN ON THE RIVER ROAD, SOUTH OF READING,
BERKS COUNTY

PLATE 101

Barn near West Chester, Chester County

Barn near Oregon, Lancaster County

PLATE 102

BARN BETWEEN SINKING SPRING AND VINEMONT, BERKS COUNTY

BARN NEAR BRICKERVILLE, LANCASTER COUNTY

PLATE 103

BARN BETWEEN MORTONVILLE AND UNIONVILLE, CHESTER COUNTY

BARN, GRAEME PARK, MONTGOMERY COUNTY

PLATE 104

FRONT ELEVATION

REAR ELEVATION

BARN BETWEEN READING AND JOANNA, BERKS COUNTY

PLATE 105

See Measured Drawing, Plate 152

FRONT ELEVATION

See Measured Drawing, Plate 152

REAR ELEVATION

BARN NEAR ANSELMA ON THE OLD CONESTOGA ROAD, CHESTER COUNTY

PLATE 106

BARN BRIDGE, CHESTER COUNTY

BARN AT JUNCTION OF OLD CONESTOGA AND SWEDESFORD ROADS, CHESTER COUNTY

BARN ON THE RIDGE ROAD NEAR KNAUERTOWN, CHESTER COUNTY

FOREBAY ON BARN BETWEEN MORTONVILLE AND MARSHALLTON, CHESTER COUNTY

PLATE 107

FOREBAY OF BARN NEAR LENAPE, CHESTER COUNTY

BARN AT HOWELLVILLE,
CHESTER COUNTY

BARN NEAR CHESTER SPRINGS,
CHESTER COUNTY

PLATE 108

CHESTER COUNTY

BUCKS COUNTY

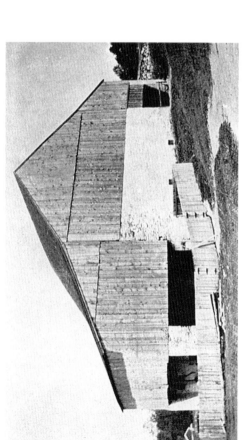

CHESTER COUNTY

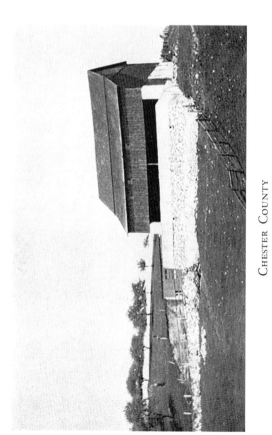

CHESTER COUNTY

VARIOUS BARNS

Plate 109

Barn near Newtown Square, Chester County

Barn on the River Road near Reading, Berks County

PLATE 110

FOREBAY OF BARN NEAR GOODVILLE,
LANCASTER COUNTY

FOREBAY OF BARN BETWEEN BLACKHORSE AND COMPASS,
CHESTER COUNTY

PLATE 111

DECORATED BARN, LEHIGH COUNTY

BARN NEAR KUTZTOWN, BERKS COUNTY

PLATE 112

BERKS COUNTY

BERKS COUNTY

LANCASTER COUNTY

PLATE 113

BARN ON THE CONESTOGA CREEK NEAR AKRON, LANCASTER COUNTY

BARN AT CHURCHTOWN, LANCASTER COUNTY

PLATE 114

BARN DOOR HOODS CHARACTERISTIC OF BUCKS COUNTY

PLATE 115

BARN DOOR HOODS CHARACTERISTIC OF BUCKS COUNTY

PLATE 116

LEBANON COUNTY

BERKS COUNTY

LIME KILN

BUCKS COUNTY

LANCASTER COUNTY

DETAILS OF STONE WORK

PLATE 117

CHESTER COUNTY

CHESTER COUNTY

LANCASTER COUNTY

CHIMNEY FOUNDATIONS

PLATE 118

BIRD IN HAND MEETING HOUSE, LANCASTER COUNTY

CHESTER COUNTY

MARSHALLTON MEETING HOUSE, CHESTER COUNTY

UPPING BLOCKS

PLATE 119

GATES, FENCES AND AN ARBOR

PLATE 120

CHESTER COUNTY

LANCASTER COUNTY   CHESTER COUNTY

FENCES

PLATE 121

BERKS COUNTY

BOX CORNICES

LANCASTER COUNTY

PLATE 122

PLASTER COVE CORNICE, BERKS COUNTY

See Measured Drawing, Plate 157

CORNICE FRAMING, JOHN CHADDS BARN, CHESTER COUNTY

CORNICE DETAILS

PLATE 123

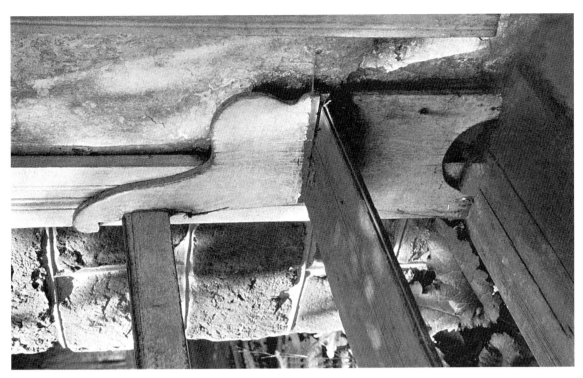

BERKS COUNTY

PORCH DETAILS

LEBANON COUNTY

PLATE 124

See Measured Drawing, Plate 156

DOORWAY, CHESTER COUNTY

DOORWAY, MARSHALLTON MEETING HOUSE,
CHESTER COUNTY

PLATE 125

BERKS COUNTY

SHEATHING DOORS

LANCASTER COUNTY

PLATE 126

BERKS COUNTY

CHESTER COUNTY

ENTRANCE TO SPRING ROOM, CHESTER COUNTY

ENTRANCE TO COVE, LANCASTER COUNTY

BARN DOORS

PLATE 127

SHUTTERS OPEN

SHUTTERS CLOSED

SHUTTERS, THE CLOISTER, EPHRATA, LANCASTER COUNTY

Plate 128

Shutters, Mennonite Meeting House, Landisville, Lancaster County

Shutters, Moravian Settlement, Bethlehem

PLATE 129

EARLY DOMESTIC ARCHITECTURE OF PENNSYLVANIA

SHUTTERS, BROWN HOUSE, PEACH BOTTOM, LANCASTER COUNTY

PLATE 130

WINDOW AND SHUTTERS, HOPE LODGE, WHITEMARSH, MONTGOMERY COUNTY

PLATE 131

See Measured Drawing, Plate 158

LANCASTER COUNTY

YORK COUNTY

BERKS COUNTY

BERKS COUNTY

PUMPS

PLATE 132

CHESTER COUNTY   LANCASTER COUNTY

BERKS COUNTY   LANCASTER COUNTY

PUMPS

PLATE 133

OLD STILL NEAR KUTZTOWN, BERKS COUNTY

MEASURED DRAWINGS

PLATE 134

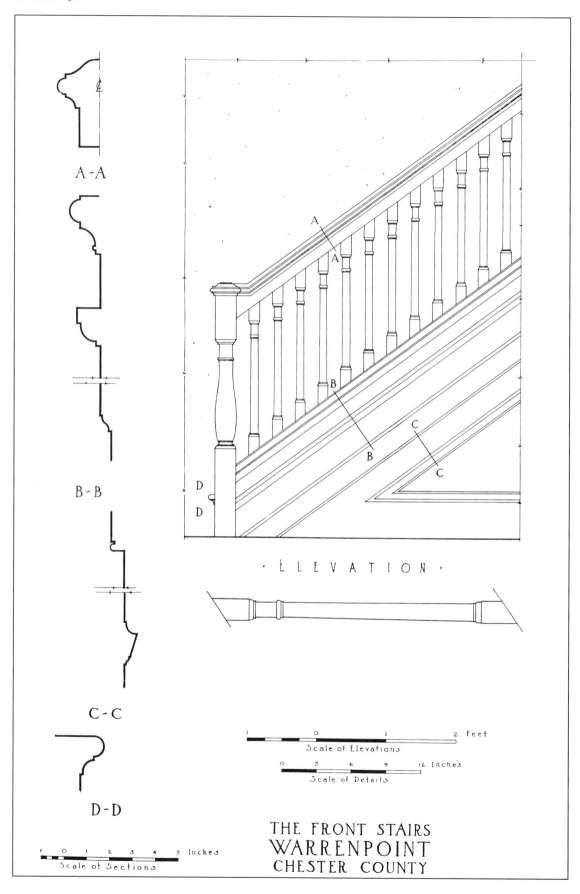

A-A

B-B

C-C

D-D

· E L E V A T I O N ·

1 0 1 2 Feet
Scale of Elevations

0 3 6 9 12 Inches
Scale of Details

1 0 1 2 3 4 5 Inches
Scale of Sections

THE FRONT STAIRS
WARRENPOINT
CHESTER COUNTY

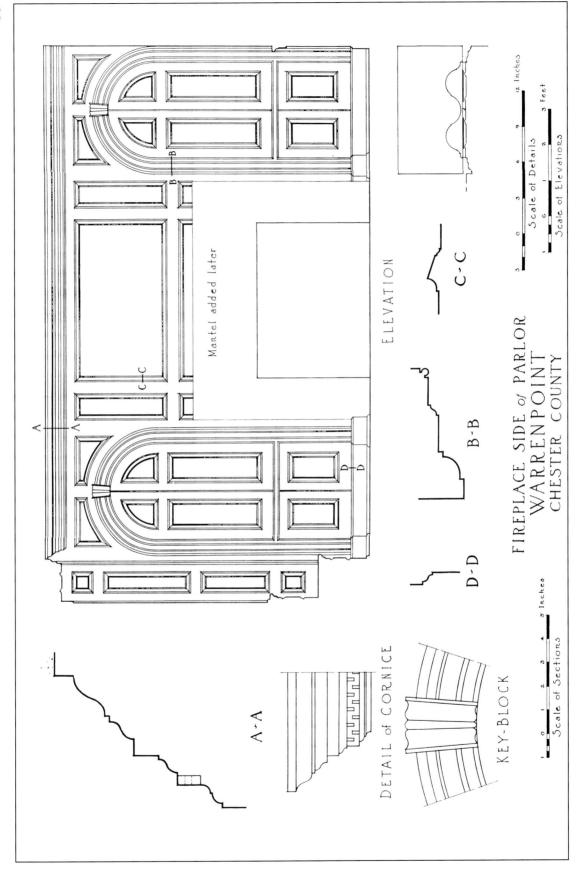

PLATE 135

Mantel added later

ELEVATION

C-C

B-B

D-D

FIREPLACE SIDE of PARLOR
WARRENPOINT
CHESTER COUNTY

A-A

DETAIL of CORNICE

KEY-BLOCK

Scale of Details

Scale of Elevations

12 Inches

3 Feet

Scale of Sections

5 Inches

PLATE 136

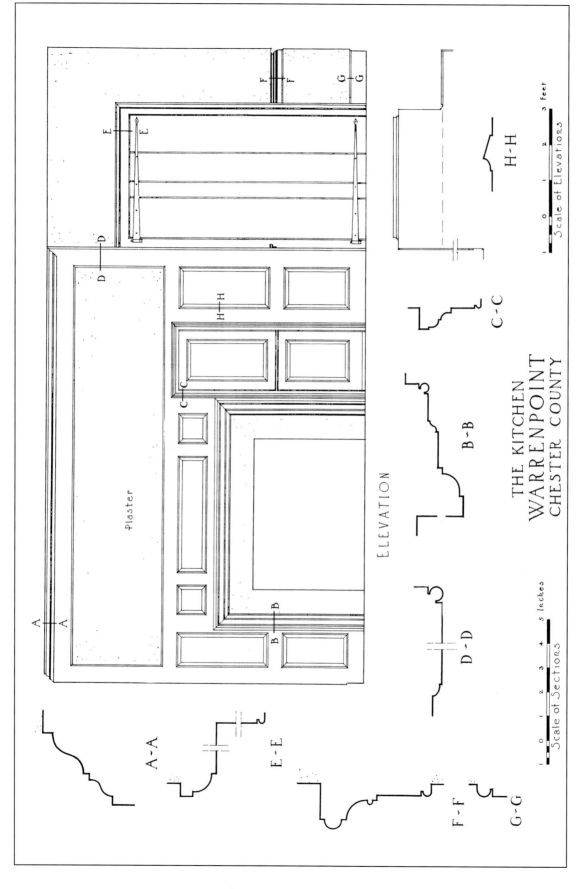

Plaster

A~A

E~E

F~F

G~G

ELEVATION

D~D

B~B

C~C

H~H

THE KITCHEN
WARRENPOINT
CHESTER COUNTY

Scale of Sections

Scale of Elevations

PLATE 137

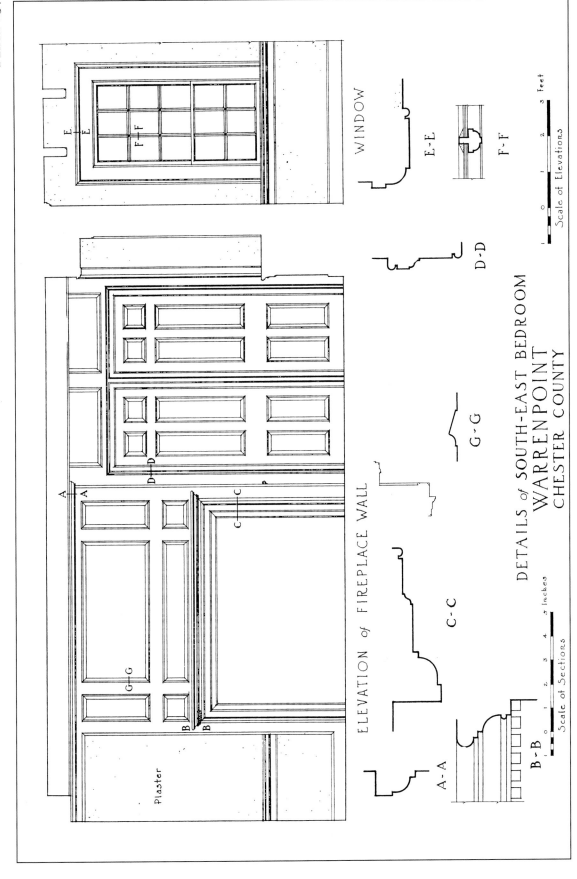

WINDOW

E-E

F-F

D-D

G-G

C-C

A-A

B-B

ELEVATION of FIREPLACE WALL

Plaster

Scale of Elevations

Scale of Sections

DETAILS of SOUTH-EAST BEDROOM
WARRENPOINT
CHESTER COUNTY

PLATE 138

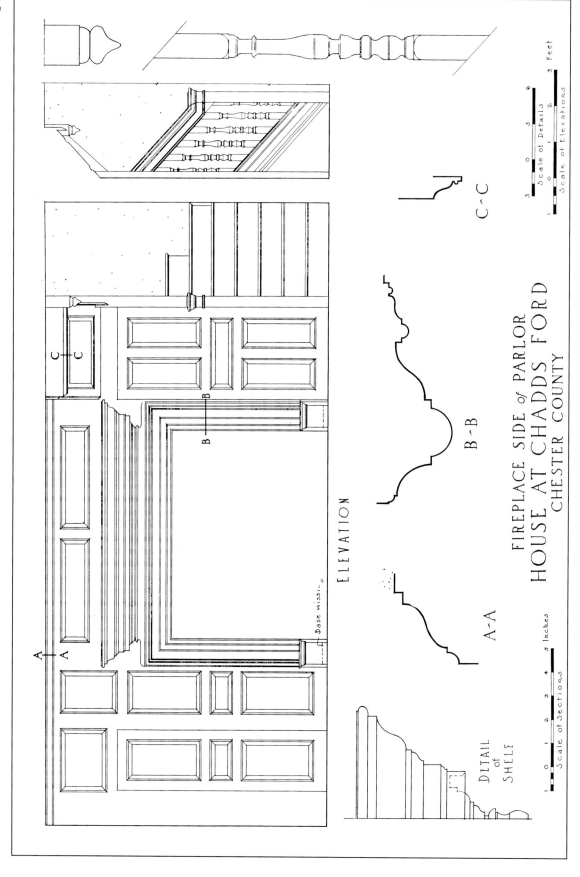

ELEVATION

A-A

B-B

C-C

DETAIL
of
SHELF

Base Missing

FIREPLACE SIDE of PARLOR
HOUSE AT CHADDS FORD
CHESTER COUNTY

Scale of Details
Scale of Elevations
Scale of Sections
Inches
Feet

PLATE 139

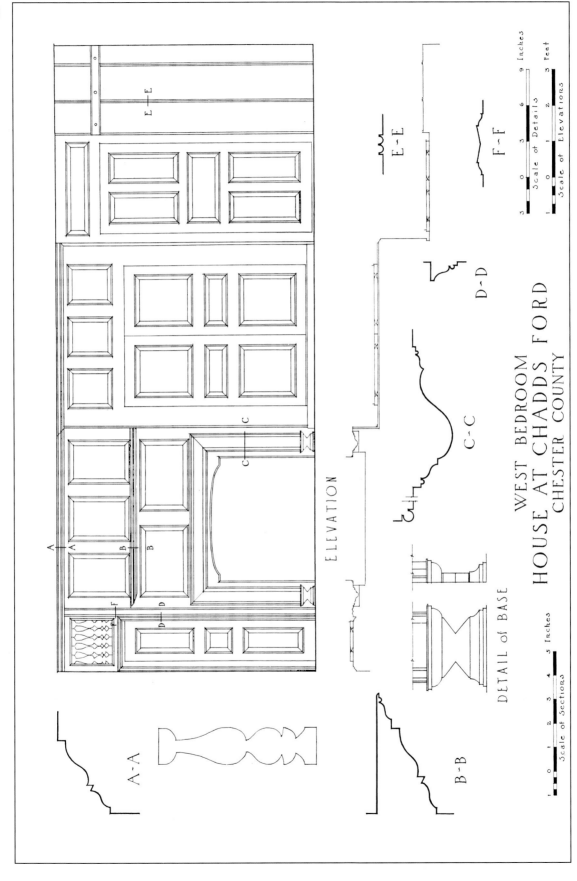

ELEVATION

A-A

B-B

C-C

D-D

E-E

F-F

DETAIL of BASE

WEST BEDROOM
HOUSE AT CHADDS FORD
CHESTER COUNTY

Scale of Sections

Scale of Details

Scale of Elevations

PLATE 140

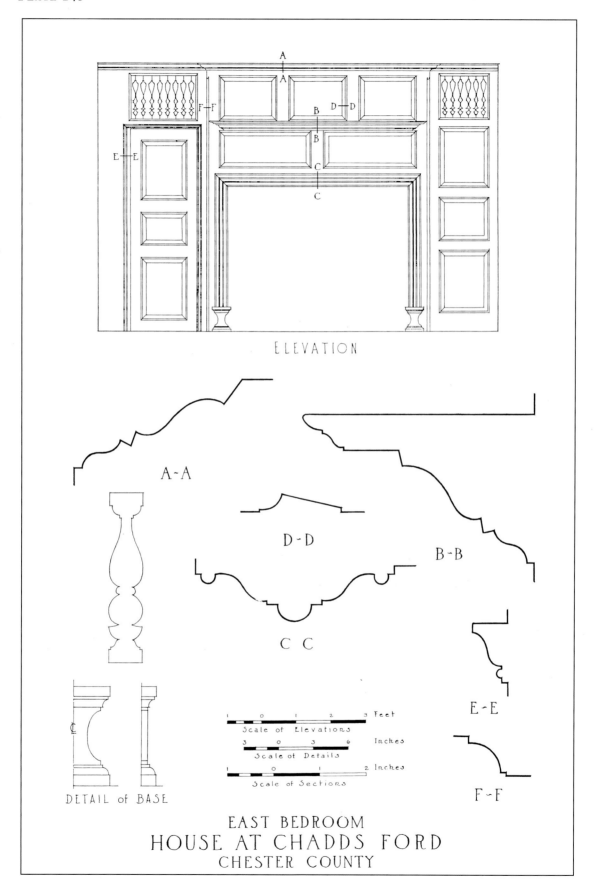

ELEVATION

A~A

D~D

B~B

C C

E~E

DETAIL of BASE

F~F

Scale of Elevations

Scale of Details

Scale of Sections

EAST BEDROOM
HOUSE AT CHADDS FORD
CHESTER COUNTY

PLATE 141

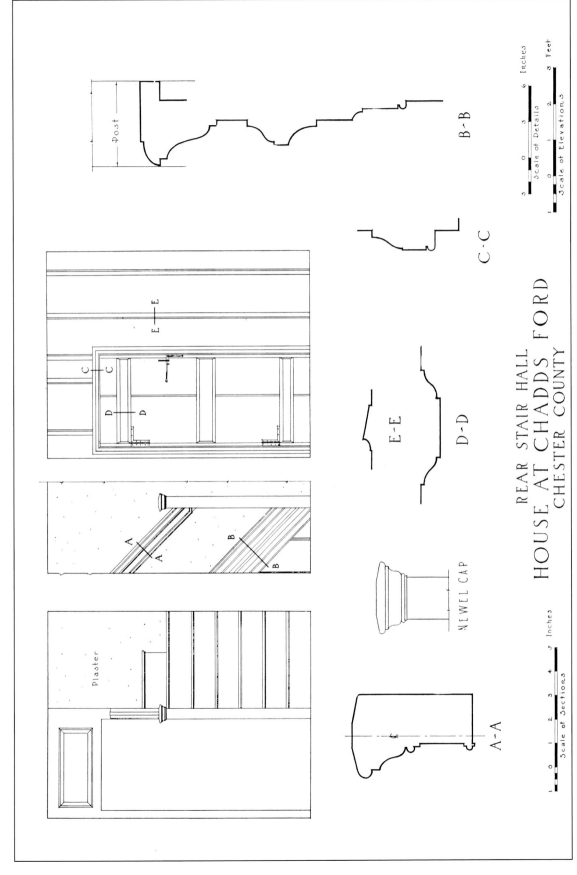

Post

B-B

C-C

E-E

E-E

D-D

NEWEL CAP

Plaster

A-A

REAR STAIR HALL
HOUSE AT CHADDS FORD
CHESTER COUNTY

Scale of Details

Scale of Elevations

Scale of Sections

PLATE 142

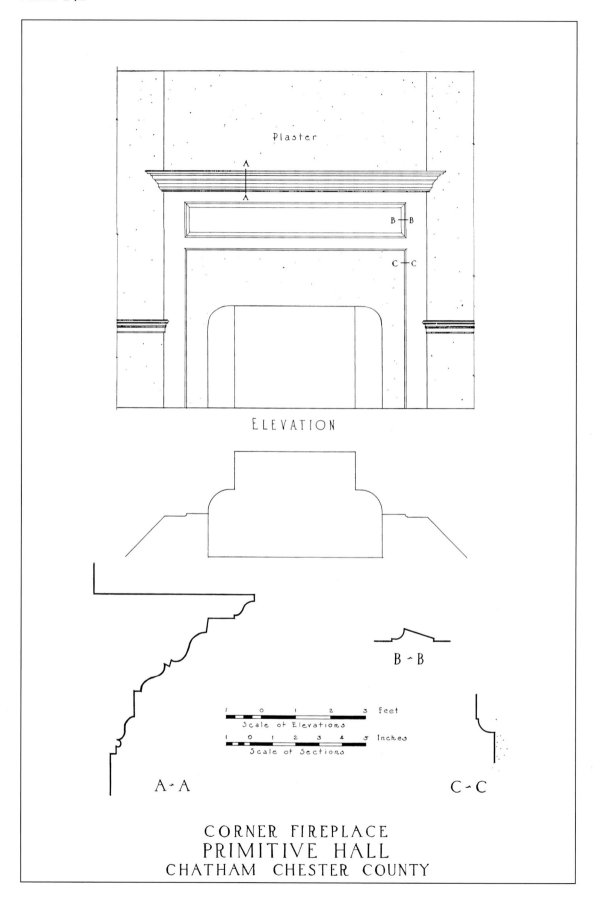

Plaster

ELEVATION

B - B

0 1 2 3 Feet
Scale of Elevations
0 1 2 3 4 5 Inches
Scale of Sections

A - A

C - C

CORNER FIREPLACE
PRIMITIVE HALL
CHATHAM CHESTER COUNTY

PLATE 143

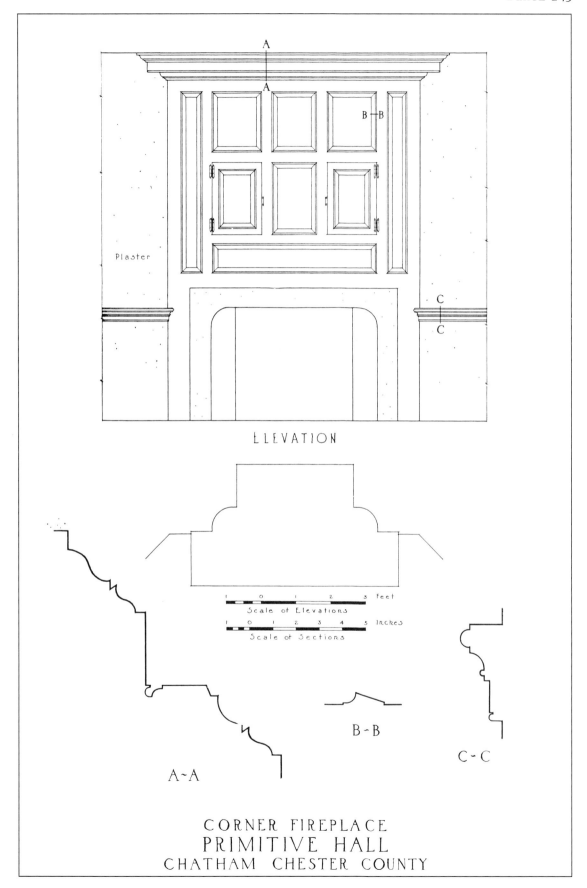

ELEVATION

A~A

B-B

C-C

Plaster

1   0   1   2   3 Feet
Scale of Elevations

1   0   1   2   3   4   5 Inches
Scale of Sections

CORNER FIREPLACE
PRIMITIVE HALL
CHATHAM CHESTER COUNTY

PLATE 144

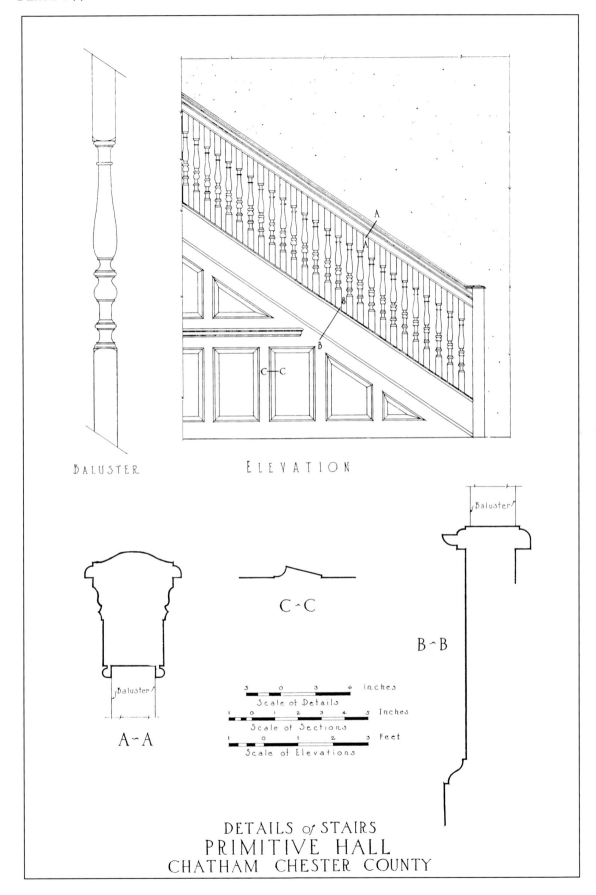

BALUSTER   ELEVATION

C~C

A~A

B~B

3 0 3 6 inches
Scale of Details
1 0 1 2 3 4 5 Inches
Scale of Sections
1 0 1 2 3 Feet
Scale of Elevations

DETAILS of STAIRS
PRIMITIVE HALL
CHATHAM CHESTER COUNTY

PLATE 145

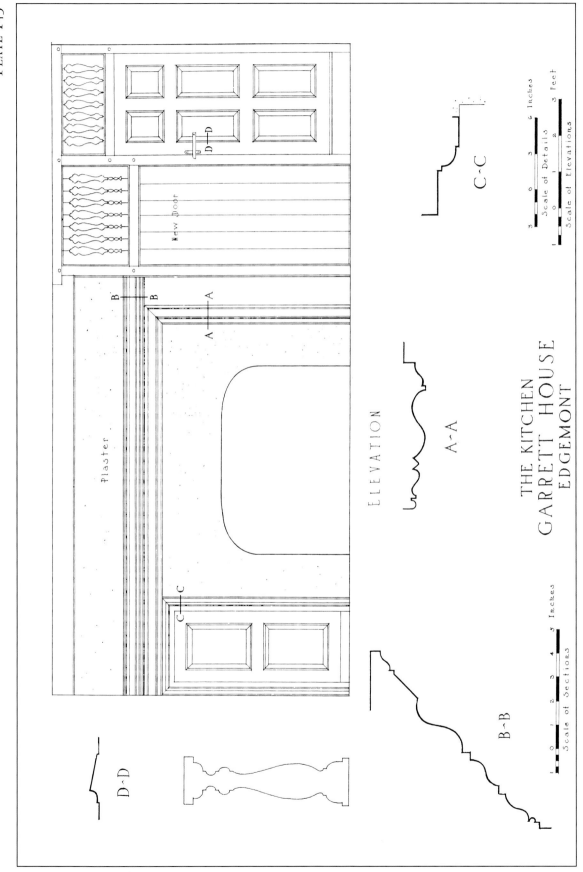

New Door

Plaster

ELEVATION

A~A

C~C

B~B

D~D

Scale of Details
Scale of Elevations

Scale of Sections

THE KITCHEN
GARRETT HOUSE
EDGEMONT

PLATE 146

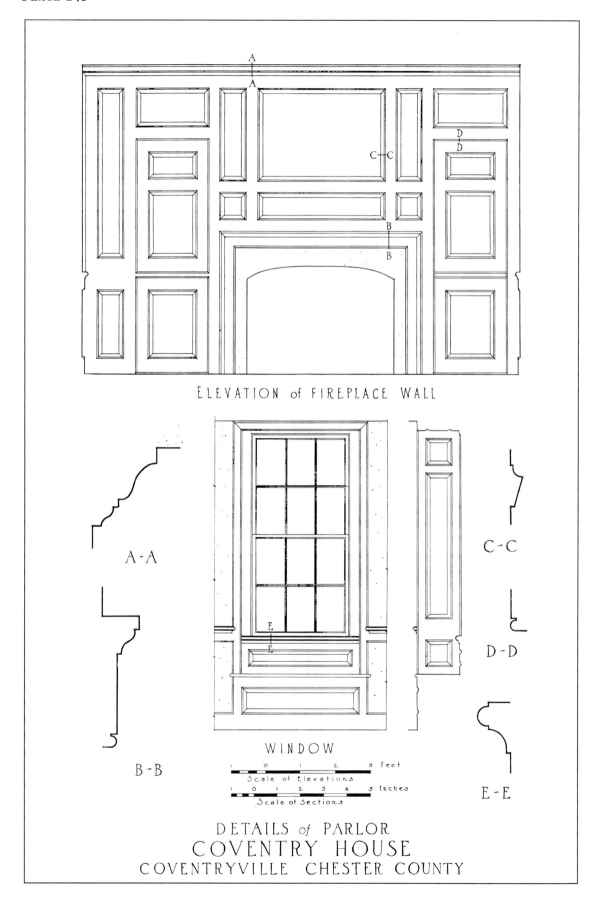

ELEVATION of FIREPLACE WALL

A-A

B-B

C-C

D-D

E-E

WINDOW

Scale of Elevations
Scale of Sections

DETAILS of PARLOR
COVENTRY HOUSE
COVENTRYVILLE CHESTER COUNTY

PLATE 147

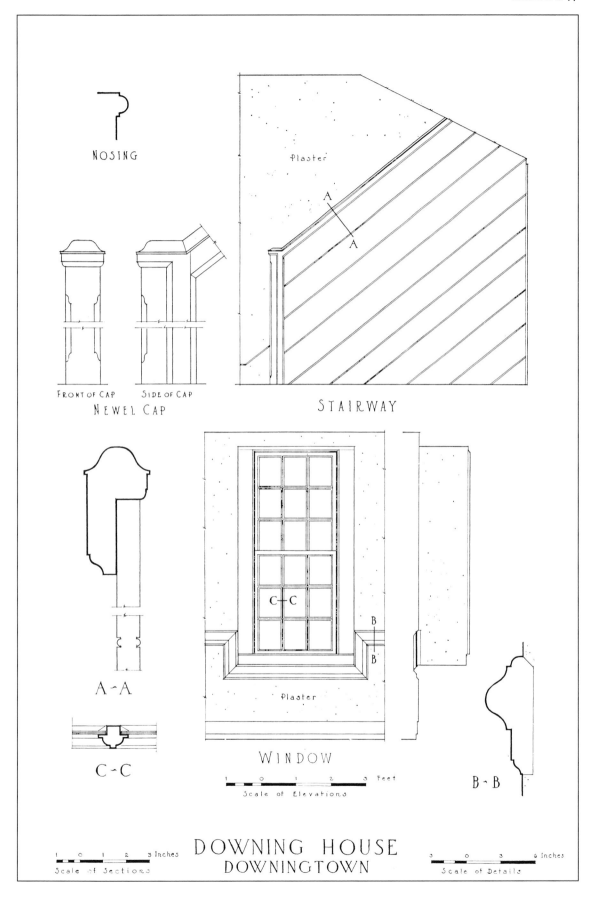

NOSING

FRONT OF CAP   SIDE OF CAP
NEWEL CAP

Plaster

STAIRWAY

A – A

C – C

Plaster

WINDOW

B – B

1   0   1   2   3 Feet
Scale of Elevations

DOWNING HOUSE
DOWNINGTOWN

1   0   1   2   3 Inches
Scale of Sections

3   0   3   6 Inches
Scale of Details

PLATE 148

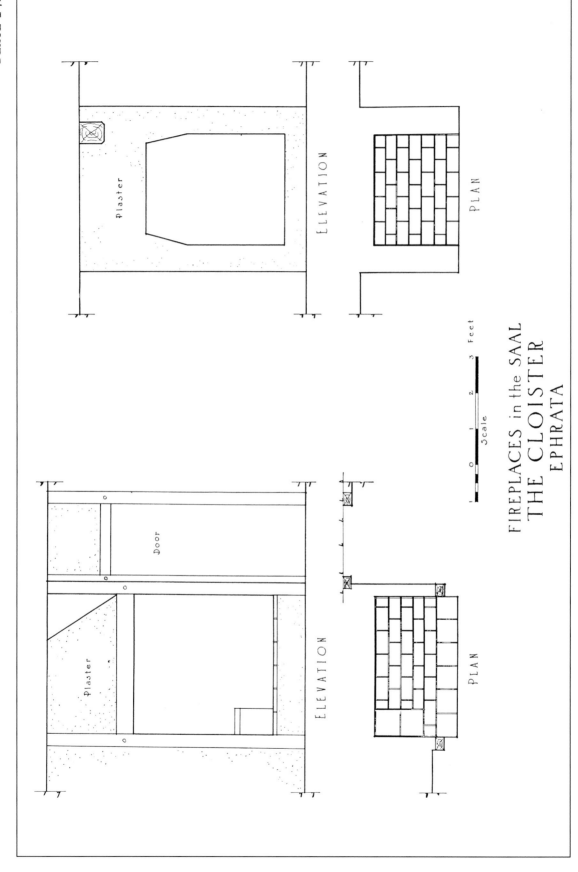

ELEVATION

PLAN

ELEVATION

PLAN

Plaster

Door

Plaster

Scale
Feet

FIREPLACES in the SAAL
THE CLOISTER
EPHRATA

PLATE 149

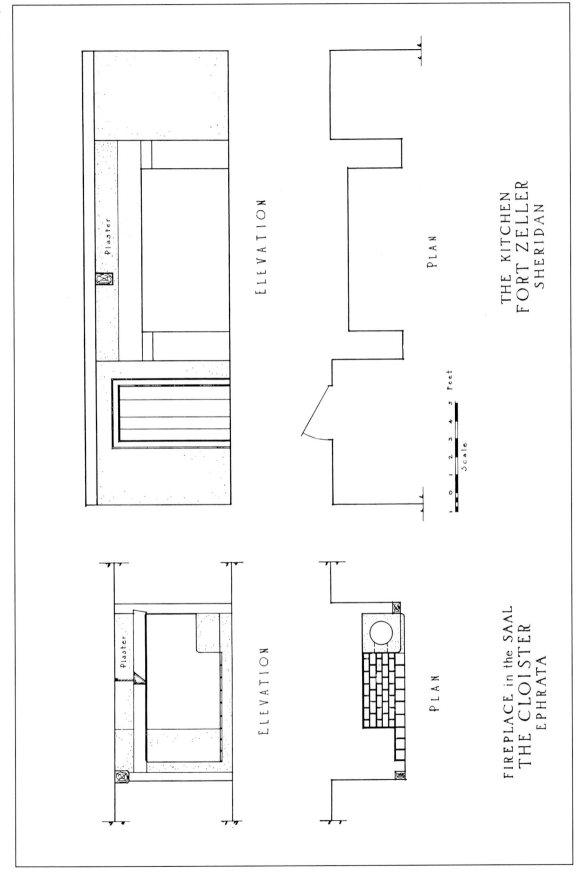

ELEVATION

PLASTER

PLAN

THE KITCHEN
FORT ZELLER
SHERIDAN

ELEVATION

Plaster

PLAN

FIREPLACE in the SAAL
THE CLOISTER
EPHRATA

0 1 2 3 4 5 Feet
Scale

PLATE 150

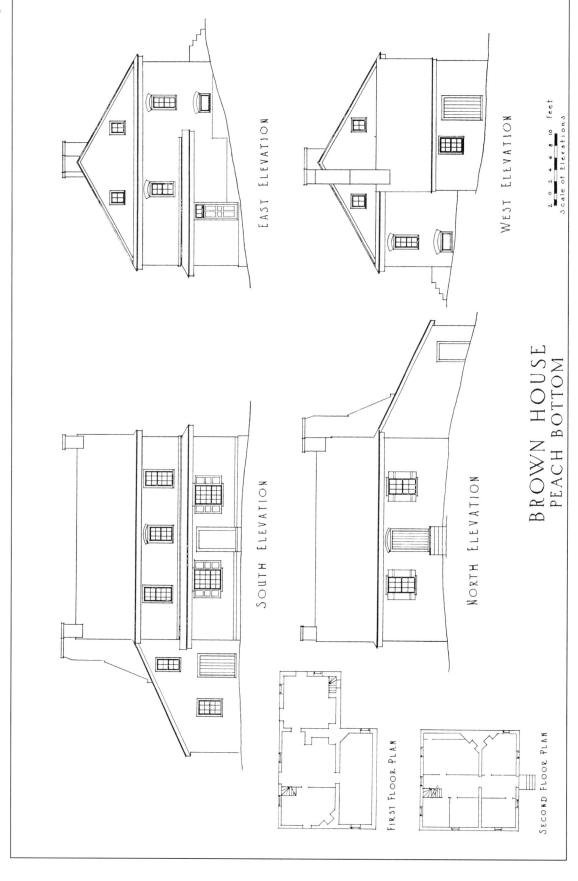

EAST ELEVATION

WEST ELEVATION

2 0 2 4 6 8 10 Feet
Scale of Elevations

SOUTH ELEVATION

NORTH ELEVATION

FIRST FLOOR PLAN

SECOND FLOOR PLAN

BROWN HOUSE
PEACH BOTTOM

Plate 151

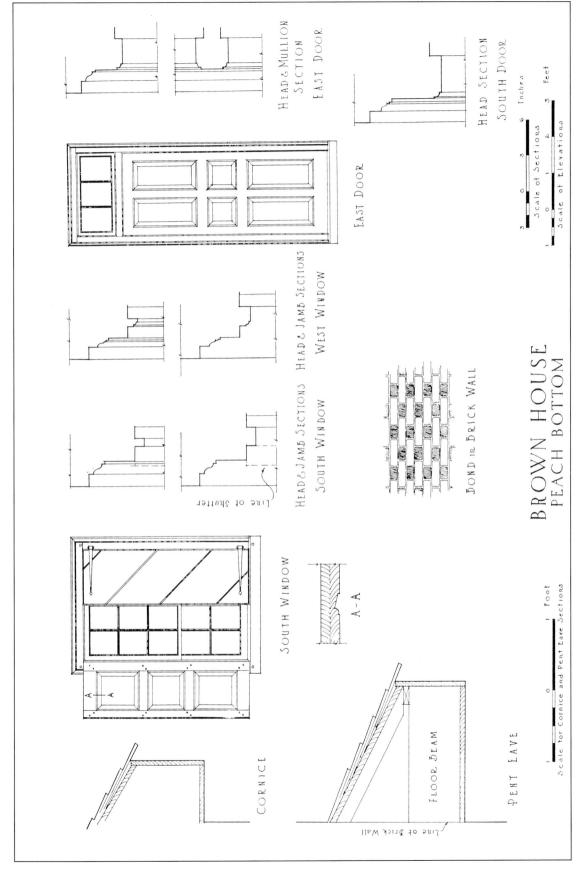

Head & Mullion Section
East Door

East Door

Head Section
South Door

Inches
Scale of Sections
Scale of Elevations

Head & Jamb Sections
West Window

Head & Jamb Sections
South Window

Line of Shutter

Bond in Brick Wall

BROWN HOUSE
PEACH BOTTOM

South Window

A-A

Cornice

Floor Beam

Pent Eave

Line of Brick Wall

Foot
Scale for Cornice and Pent Eave Sections

PLATE 152

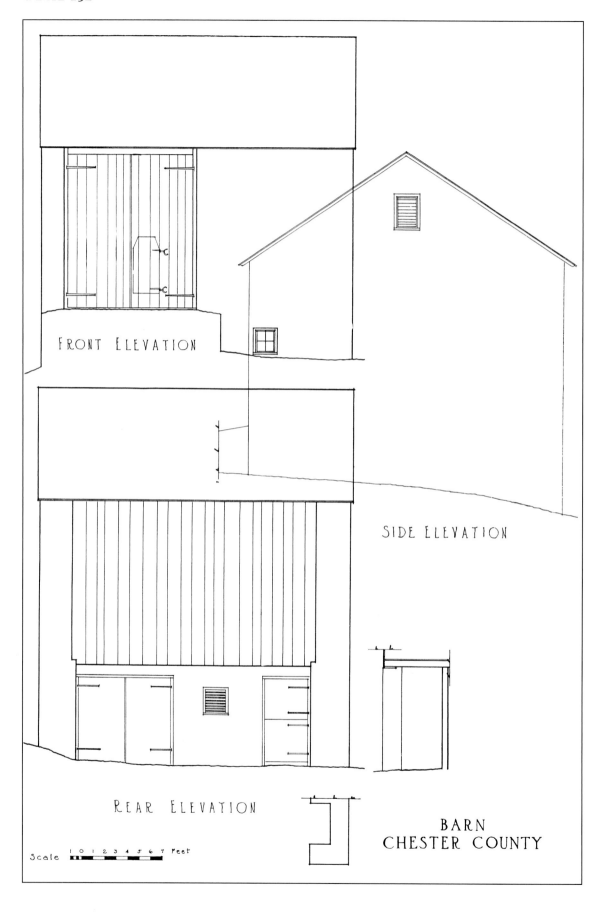

FRONT ELEVATION

SIDE ELEVATION

REAR ELEVATION

Scale 1 0 1 2 3 4 5 6 7 Feet

BARN
CHESTER COUNTY

PLATE 153

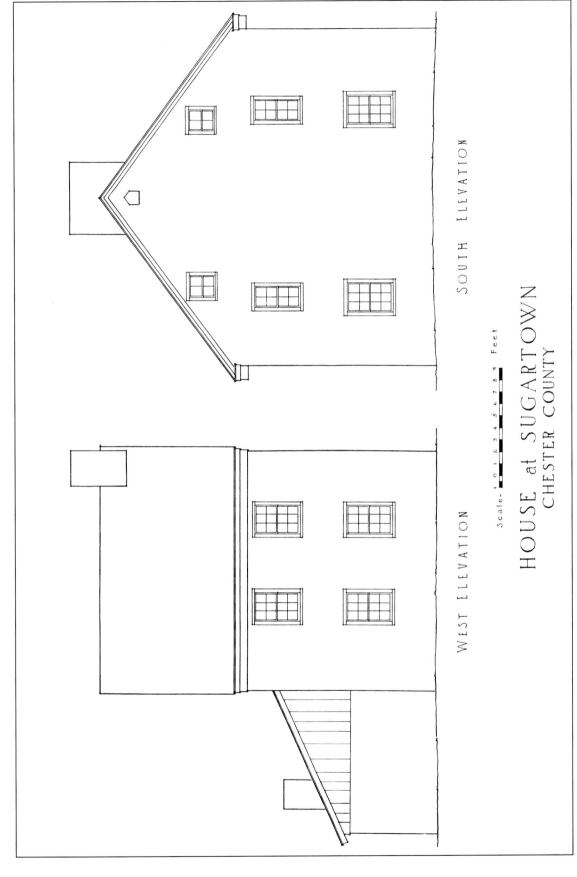

SOUTH ELEVATION

WEST ELEVATION

Scale- 1 0 1 2 3 4 5 6 7 8 9 Feet

HOUSE at SUGARTOWN
CHESTER COUNTY

PLATE 154

SIDE ELEVATION

FRONT ELEVATION

Scale

HOUSE near DOWNINGTOWN

PLATE 155

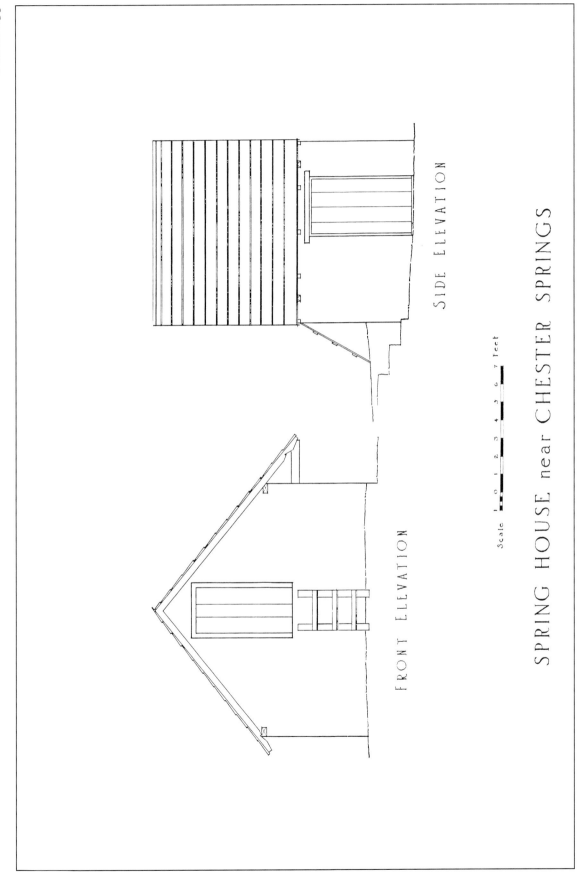

SIDE ELEVATION

FRONT ELEVATION

Scale

SPRING HOUSE near CHESTER SPRINGS

PLATE 156

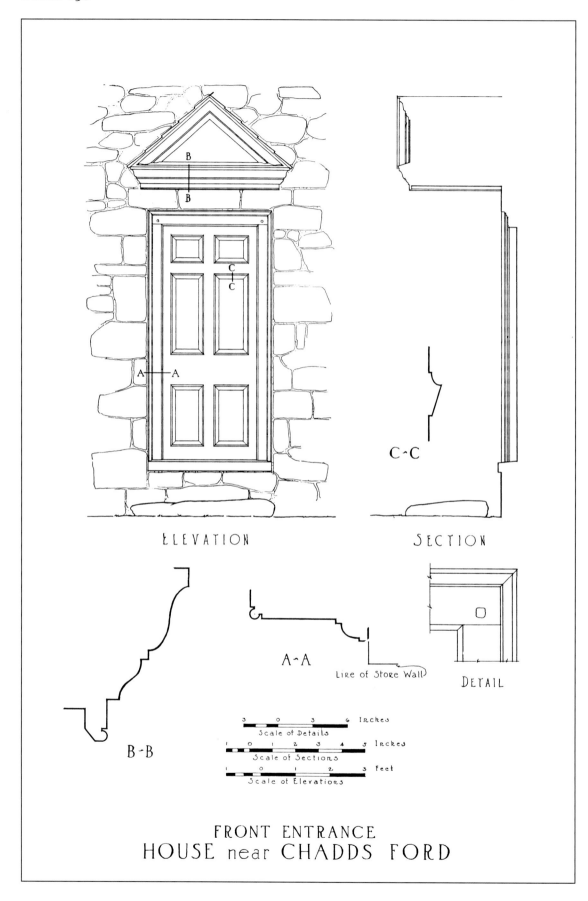

ELEVATION

SECTION

C-C

B-B

A-A

Line of Stone Wall

DETAIL

Scale of Details

Scale of Sections

Scale of Elevations

FRONT ENTRANCE
HOUSE near CHADDS FORD

PLATE 157

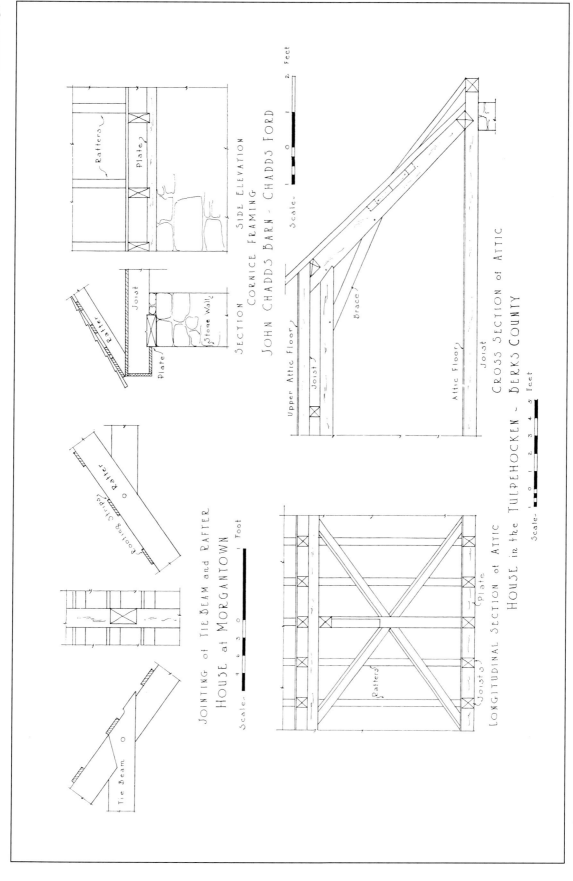

Rafters

Plate

SIDE ELEVATION

Joist

Rafter

Stone Wall

Plate

SECTION   CORNICE FRAMING

JOHN CHADDS BARN - CHADDS FORD

Scale- 0   1   2 Feet

Rafter

Roofing Strips

JOINTING of TIE BEAM and RAFTER
HOUSE at MORGANTOWN

Scale- 9 6 3 0   1 Foot

Tie Beam

Upper Attic Floor

Joist

Brace

Attic Floor

Joist

CROSS SECTION of ATTIC

Plate

Rafters

Joists

LONGITUDINAL SECTION of ATTIC

HOUSE in the TULPEHOCKEN - BERKS COUNTY

Scale- 1 0 1 2 3 4 5 Feet

PLATE 158

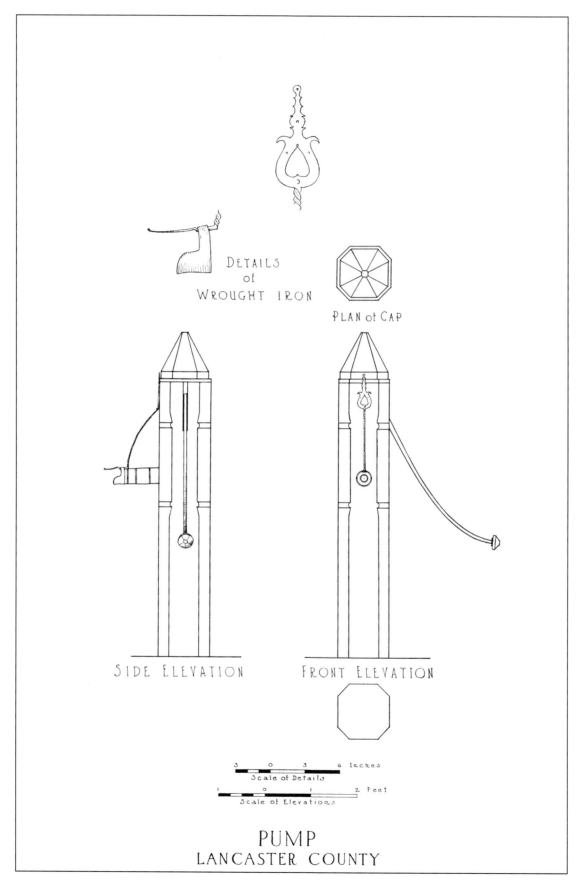

DETAILS
of
WROUGHT IRON

PLAN of CAP

SIDE ELEVATION

FRONT ELEVATION

3   0   3   6 Inches
Scale of Details

1   0   1   2 Feet
Scale of Elevations

PUMP
LANCASTER COUNTY